1

Trust the Process

"Move with the money, but at the speed of opportunity."

-Clifford "TI" Harris

Trust- according to Webster's Collegiate Dictionary means 1.assured hope. 2. Depends 3. Hope 4. Have faith in.

In this case the definition of the word is used as a verb, showing action.

Process- serious actions or operations directed toward a result.

I think the definition of both words are so fitting.

Thank you for purchasing this book, the 2nd of 5 books I am releasing over the course of my entrepreneurial journey. If you have the previous book, you already know I write these alongside my own progression as I am being coached or advised by my mentor.

So here we are in the 4th year of my journey as a business owner and entrepreneur. This is after the idea, crossing all the T's and dotting the I's. You are making a little money. The never ending questions always comes up:

1. *What should I do now?*
2. *Can I make more money?*
3. *How do I scale?*
4. *How do I increase my online presence?*
5. *Do I move to a building? More space, more inventory?*

Etc. etc.

30% of businesses fail during the first 2 years of opening. 50% the first 5 years. 66% fail the first 10. According to the SBA only 25% of new businesses make it to 15 years or more. Now the 6 reasons SBA list are: 1. Leadership, 2-lack of uniqueness, & value, 3- not in touch with customers, 4- unprofitable, 5- poor money management, 6- rapid growth & over expansion.

FORGET ALL OF THAT!!! Businesses fail because BOs (Business Owners), are still trying to conduct business the traditional way.

When I started getting serious about business, I wanted to share all of the new insider tips my mentor was feeding me. I mean this is the info the upper 1%ers of the wealthy keep close to their chest because they are guaranteed to get you to where you want to be in life and financial status. It's generally not put into the hands of the 99% unless they recognise something special in you. Oftentimes they will just offer you a large check and buy you out.

So, I'm sharing my hot tips, which I call GOLDEN NUGGETS of information in a social media group I am a member of, and this crafter immediately started ragging me about how it was not going to work. He's been in business for 30 years blah, blah, blah....

Thinking back I wonder what would've happened if I had allowed that person to turn my mind back toward following the sheep (sleep). I'm glad I didn't and here's why.

One of the best pieces of advice I ever received was, "if you want to drive a Lamborghini don't listen to someone who drives a Ford. If a person has been in business 30 years and topped out at 100k, the answer is simple and obvious. They are comfortable right where they are, or they don't know how to scale for more. Did you know that there are still people who believe a computer of the devil?,
They can't send an email, pay bills or order online because there is someone out to steal their identity. They

are stuck, not set in their ways. They can't see the forest for staring at one tree.

I have learned over the last 4 years that there are people in this world that just want to go through life and die safely.

If there is one thing I want you to always remember is that, "Move with the money at the speed of opportunity." Meaning if you want to be successful you will have to keep up with the current trends of the business world as soon as it changes. That will keep you relevant and trending with clientele. Let's start answering those questions.

What should I do now?

Year one you are a rollercoaster, Customers are riding the wave because your business is brand new. Trust me, it will appear as your product or service is the best thing since the invention of cars. You should pay close attention to your peak and low times during the year. What product/service customers are buying on repeat. Which ones are moving slowly or not at all. Year one will feel like a rush, but you must keep your eyes wide open on every aspect of the business.

Going into your 2nd year you are armed with this information and applying it accordingly. Putting more emphasis on those products or services that are generating you money and building on your brand. Branding is everything in business, it's your name, as well as the product or service. The bible says,

"a good name is greater than great wealth." Prov. 22:1.

This is the year your customers should be giving your company referrals, or referring your company to other potential clients. And you should reward those who do.

Look into giving gift cards or certificates to customers/clients who refer to your product or service. Everybody loves a gift. Even the smallest of appreciating gestures speaks volumes. In my company I give away a free leather key fob, or leather bracelet. I want my customers/clients to be draped in my products. That's a walking billboard of advertising for Premier Leather Crafters. Plus it gives them a chance to glimpse into my inventory. This way birthdays, anniversaries, graduations, weddings, or any other event you can think of they will call me for those one of a kind items you can't just buy from your everyday retailer.

Year one also should tell you when to run sales or ad campaigns on social media in my case.

What's my next Move?

Social media, social media, social media. SOCIAL MEDIA!!!!!!!! If you are not plugged into every social media outlet there is, then you should. Let me run down a list of the platforms I am currently running on: Facebook, Instagram, Twitter, LinkedIn, Flickr, Tumblr, YouTube & Google. Although YouTube & Google are not social media platforms, they are free to set up a page and make money.

Here's some fun facts you should know, and why I utilize social media outlets to run my business. According to the Nielsen report, the average American watches five hours and 4 minutes of TV everyday. 35 hours a week, 77 days a year that is 5 hours less than a regular schedule work week.

Now the amount of time a person is plugged into the internet and social media outlets. Social media is an inseparable part of our everyday lives. It is always there, from the moment we wake up until we fall asleep with our phone in hand.

But how much time do people spend on social media? And which apps get the most attention?

The answer to the latter is probably obvious to anyone with an online presence. Apps like Facebook, Twitter, Instagram, YouTube, SnapChat, WhatsApp, and Facebook Messenger have become almost synonymous with the term "social media".

Impressive, considering there are **3.196 billion people** actively using these networks. What's more, the internet user of today spends an average of **2 hours and 22 minutes** socializing online, and most of it happens on these six most popular platforms.

According to GlobalWebIndex, Philippines residents lead the way with **3 hours and 57 minutes** a day on social media channels. Second place goes to the Brazilians with **3 hours and 39 minutes**. Last are the Japanese with only **48 minutes** of social media time.

Between April and September of 2018, **83% of all internet-users** were engaged with social media. And only **24%** of those find it has a positive effect on their work.

Facebook

In 2019, **3.48 billion people use social media**, and **2.23 billion of them** are active monthly users on Facebook.

The biggest social media platform is mainly used for networking. However, media watching has always been a part of Facebook – be it uploading a photo or streaming a video, we still spend a lot of time on the site.

An eMarketer research shows Americans (aged 18+) spend **43 minutes** per day on Facebook. This is a **seven-minute** from 2014. It usually consists of one longer visit and lots of shorter ones.

In 2018, the average time spent on the mobile Facebook app was around **58 minutes** a day.

This doesn't come as a surprise, as **95.1% of all Facebook visitors** access it through mobile devices. The network is a big part of why the daily average time spent on a phone gets higher every year.

Part of this is due to the **2,055 billion active users** that now access the network through their smartphone or tablet. Scrolling through your newsfeed has become possible virtually anywhere. There are even **10 million active accounts** on feature phones.

In comparison, only **31.8% (687 million) unique accounts** check Facebook from a laptop and/or a PC exclusively.

Since November 2018, Android and iOS users can check how much time they spend on the network with the "Your Time on Facebook" app as well. You can find it under the Settings and Privacy tab.

It can also tell you if you spend more time than your peers there. It is there to remind you that there's life beyond Facebook.

YouTube

YouTube maintains a solid second place in the "most used social media" category.

79% of all internet users own a YouTube account (Facebook sitting at 85%). However, the video and streaming platform has the most active users – **86% of all people on the Web visit it actively**.

The majority of them point out entertainment as their main reason to visit the site.

In other news, Futuresource Consulting data from 2016 has some interesting points regarding UK users, aged 3-16. According to them, a tad over **10% of them** watch more than **3 hours** of YouTube videos daily.

In addition, VAB research from 2017 shows the average person spent **1163 minutes per month** on YouTube. This equals a little over **38 minutes a day**. However, the actual *watch time* on the platform has grown by **60%** between 2016 and 2017.

I can only imagine what those results will be for 2019.

Additionally, statistics also show users prefer to watch YouTube videos on their smartphone or tablet – those account for **70% of all YouTube views**. To back that claim, YouTube stated their **1.8 billion users** spend an average of 1 hour a day watching videos on their mobile device in 2018.

Last August, the video giant gave users the option to track how much time they spend on the platform each day. Anyone can check it for themselves.

Messenger

58% of people in North America use social media to stay connected to their friends and close ones, according to GlobalWebIndex graph.

It doesn't come as a surprise, then, to see Messenger and WhatsApp having such a high usage rate. The former hosts the accounts of **72% of all internet users**, while the latter has this figure at **66%**.

There is an obvious explanation for why that is. Humans are social creatures and, as such, we need connection. With the rise of the smartphone (and tablet), reaching out to another human being is **1-2 taps away**. These apps' business model is based on an innate human desire, which is why it works so well.

Therefore, we can reasonably expect the average time spent on social media to rise further.

New information that supports this claim continues to surface – a SimilarWeb article from Q1 of 2016 says Americans were spending an average of **48.5 minutes** a day on Kakao, while their Messenger usage is registered at **9.36 minutes** per day.

Regardless, things are looking up for Facebook Messenger as well. An eMarketer article suggests an **11.8 million US user growth** for the app in the next four years. This would mean a staggering **138.1 million users** will access the app in the US alone by 2022.

Naturally, users access Messenger mainly on mobile, with a small percentage using only the desktop app. Some even use it from their Apple Watch.

WhatsApp?

Messenger may have a bigger user base in general, but WhatsApp has the most active users in recent years. **60% of all people on the Web** use WhatsApp. Whatsapp's user base in India alone is 400 million. For Messenger, this figure is at **55%**. They are both owned by Facebook, though, so what seems like competition is actually kind of a rigged race.

ExpandedRamblings estimates **2 billion minutes** worth of calls is conducted daily in WhatsApp. No surprise there, considering it is the **top messaging app in 128 countries as of 2018**.

In 2016, United States users spent an average of **28.4 minutes** a day on WhatsApp. The total user base back then was **18.8 million**. Statista estimates the number will grow to **25.6 million** in 2022.

If you've ever asked yourself "how much time do we spend on social media", well – the figures are astounding. They don't show any sign of slowing down either – social media usage (and WhatsApp's in particular) will only grow in the future.

Granted – Kik, WeChat, Kakao boast better engagement in terms of minutes in the US, **yet WhatsApp already seems like the inevitable leader among the messaging services.**

Current user engagement is not the best metric that can predict how the service will grow in the future. It's relatively easier to optimize user experience compared to attracting said users in the first place. Arguably then, the number of people using an app is a better litmus test. **With WhatsApp being the undisputed champion in this category**, chances are it will continue to grow with impressive steps.

Instagram

In June 2018, Instagram users worldwide reached **1 billion**. For those of you not counting, that was a **200+ million jump** since September 2017.

63% of all people connected to the internet have a registered Instagram account. **58%** of those are active users, making it more used than Messenger on a daily basis.

However, Instagram stats from June 2018 shed light on the astonishing app progress. **400 million active daily users** spent **53 minutes** per day on the platform – just a **5-minute** difference compared to Facebook.

When it comes to time spent on the internet, **statistics really paint a vivid picture**, don't they?

In January 2019, daily usage on Instagram averages at **15 minutes**, according to SocialPilot. Keep in mind this is an average for all users, not just the active ones.

Instagram is mostly used for entertainment, but it already has solid messaging features. Doesn't necessarily mean it will try to go after WhatsApp's market. Still, it's one more reason for users to spend more time on the platform. I'm sure that's what their CEO thinks as well.

Twitter

6% of teens in the US name Twitter as their most used social network. In January 2019, **326 million users** were active on Twitter on a monthly basis. Some **9 million less** than the summer of 2018, which can be worrisome for the platform.

A 2019 survey shares Twitter users only set aside **2.7 minutes** a day to use the site. Most visits are done via desktop (**82 million users**), while mobile falls behind with **31 million**.

In addition, three-quarters of Twitter visitors claim to use it to check the news. In a sense, we can say this social media focuses on adult users as a main demographic.

Social media platforms offer an ever-wider variety of things to do.

Social media has a powerful influence on our daily activities as well. It can affect what we buy, what we like and dislike, and which places we choose to visit.

This simple networking concept is arguably just a front for a robust marketing machine running in the background.

"How much time do people spend on social media?" then becomes important in terms of revenue.

Brands are aware that social media can make or break their business, and they are using it anyway they can.

With this much money to make, these apps will keep growing – that much is certain. Use them right, and you'll find yourself with a powerful tool to uplift and inspire.

Now that you are armed with more "Golden Nuggets" of information on social media platforms, you should start seeing the value of building your brand there.

Let's be honest, if you had a traditional business, in a traditional building, selling the traditional way, you would never have 3 billion people per day come into your establishment and spend on average 3 hours.

Now you understand why you should not listen to a Ford driver when you want to drive a Lamborghini. The person I mentioned earlier was stuck in the same rut of business from 20 years ago. Now wonder he topped out at 100k. Don't get me wrong $100k is nothing to sneeze at, but least break that figure down. Taxes off the rip. Mortgage 2nd. Insurance & utilities are next. Then loans, debtors, & vendors. Employees, if any. Finally the business owner. Just tossing around some figures in my head looks like you'll be bringing home $30-45k annually with a business owner title.

How to keep the Cash Stream flowing?

This will probably be one of the shortest chapters you have or will ever read. Actually it's taking me longer to write this than give you the answer.

My mentor told me once, his first million was his hardest. Becoming a millionaire was not in my purview since I was only making roughly $25k annually. To me, it would've been easier to wrangle a purple unicorn.

As I sat there listening to how he duplicated success year after year, it finally hit me. The one common denominator of all those years was', ***"REPEAT YEAR ONE!"***

That is the answer. You simply repeat what you did in year one. Everything.

Remember the intensity, the tenacity, the drive, the laser focused mindset, the me against the world attitude you had when you first jump on the entrepreneur train? The way to keep that feeling alive is to repeat every action, every step.

This should move a lot smoother. More fluid, because you are armed with more knowledge than you had before. It reminds me of cooking. The first few times you may need to read the recipe, but after committing it to memory and repeating the process again and again, now it doesn't take as long to prepare dinner and ironically the taste improves. Why because everybody's taste is different and the creator of the recipe made it for their particular taste and flare.

Business owners and entrepreneurs must put their own spin on ideas given to them. You are not reinventing the wheel, but making the proper adjustments so the tire will fit your vehicle.

Let me share some of the things I have done. Year two, when I talked with my mentor. I was telling him business was going well, and I could barely keep up. He told me, "that was a good problem to have." HE also said I needed to take it up a notch. He suggested giving leather classes to people interested in learning to do leather crafts, i.e. teens, beginner craftsman, retirees, even go to the local VFW and teach veterans.

Another time he told me to set up a page on every social media platform, including YouTube. I should post something motivational & inspirational every day on social media. I should be making leather products every week, and record it to post on YouTube on how it's made.

Another conversation, he told me to write a book, (more on why you should write a book later.) That I should take speech classes, or join a Toastmasters group.

Now I know all of this may sound overwhelming, and at the time I was thinking the same thing, but here's a man that has a proven track record in the business world. A company with over $5 billion in sales worldwide. He has made more business owners celebrities or millionaires themselves. Investor, entrepreneur, media personality, coach, mentor developer, you name it. I said all of that to say this, why should I be afraid or doubt his advice?

My first book, I stated how he told me my company should be a $250k company, and this was the plan he was laying out for me. Step by step.

Let me break this down so you too can follow this game plan but make the proper adjustments to fit your own personal flare.

Before I do, let's get rid of all the reasons/excuses you cannot do this. ***THERE IS NOT ONE!***

Social media, YouTube, speaking engagements, workshops/seminars, even becoming an author, are all ***FREE!***

Social Media Platforms

Every social media platform is free and is an open market. Look at the statistics I listed earlier. The odds of any single business getting that kind of foot traffic, in a traditional brick and mortar business, on any given day is less than 1%. When my mentor explained this I immediately created a page on every relevant social media page. Posting something motivational or inspirational every day gave future clients and customers a look into the person I am. Social media is the new way to vet people and or businesses. Companies are now using social media pages to see if future employees are a good fit for their company, so imagine how customers are using them to see if they want to do business with you.

I cleaned up all of my social media pages, removing any thing that can be viewed as offensive or shed a negative light on my company. I don't post anything related to religion, politics, or racial issues.

All of these things are personal and should remain that way. Not to say, you can't voice your opinion but in the business, voicing your personal opinion can stop you from eating regularly. .

Since the very start of my journey, my mentor didn't care about my race, my politics, or my religion. It never came up, neither did it have an effect on whether I could perform the task set upon me. I never asked him about his. All I know is that he had the lifestyle and the freedom I wanted, and if I wanted it, I was going to do whatever he told me to do.

I found that making YouTube videos lent to my credibility as a master craftsman. Things as simple as sharing crafting techniques that other crafters wouldn't normally share boosted my subscribers and followers. I was shocked, the things I was doing for free was actually generating another cash flow stream. I was being called to put on workshops and seminars.

Through my social media platforms, I learned to create funnels or ad campaigns. The beauty in learning funnel hacks for social media is, it opens your business products or services up to millions all over the world. I've shipped products as far as Australia, Spain, and Germany. Learning how to go into the algorithms of Facebook to maximize reach for clients was a game changer. This opened up a completely different cash flow stream.

I started another business and began helping other small businesses create cash flow by teaching them the same things my mentor led me to.

Let me pause to take you back to the crafter I mentioned earlier in this book, that was stuck in the traditional ways of doing business. He was adamant that the path I set upon was not going to work. If he had used these tools, he could have easily surpassed the standstill his business was in.

Knowledge is not only power but another way to generate revenue. There are a lot of business owners, or entrepreneurs out there that have created wealth off what they know.

In urban culture, there's a saying, "the game is to be sold, and not told." There's a reason for that. There's another saying, "Give a man a fish and he'll eat for a day, but if you **TEACH** him how to fish, He'll eat forever."

What does this mean Robert? Here's what it means The reason the game is sold and not told is because if you give it away and a person does not do exactly what's told, you just wasted your time. Time is money. It's the most expensive commodity in the world. Once it's gone, it's gone. At the time of this writing, there will never be another January 4, 2020 1:35pm ever again.

If you don't teach others how to fish, or do it for self, they'll expect you to feed them forever. That's dependant. It is my aim and purpose to arm young businesses and entrepreneurs with the tools they need to provide and take care of their families, the same, as what my mentor did for me. The only difference is I had absolute trust in the information and the opportunity I was being blessed with.

My social media accounts generated revenue to springboard the launching of my Google page and my website. By establishing a Google page it opened my company up to another demographic, those customers who may or may not fully be engaged ,on social media platforms. They trust Google search engines more than social media.

About Google My Business

Google My Business is a free and easy-to-use tool for businesses and organizations to manage their online presence across Google, including Search and Maps. If you verify and edit your business information, you can both help customers find your business and tell them your story.

Benefits of Google My Business

Manage your information

Manage the information that Google users find when they search for your business, or the products and services that you offer. Businesses that verify their information with Google My Business are twice as likely to be considered reputable by consumers.1 When people find your business on Google Maps and Search, make sure they have access to information like your hours, website, and street address.

Interact with customers

Read and respond to reviews from your customers, and post photos that show off what you do. Businesses that add photos to their Business Profiles receive 42% more requests for directions on Google Maps, and 35% more clicks through to their websites than businesses that don't.

Understand and expand your presence

Find insights on how customers searched for your business, and where those customers are coming from. You can also find information like how many people called your business directly from the phone number displayed on local search results in Search and Maps. When you're ready, you can create and track the performance of Smart campaigns to spread the word about your work.

YouTube can generate another cash flow stream.

Videos are a great way to differentiate your business and stand out among your competitors online. YouTube is no longer regarded as just an entertainment site, it has grown into an invaluable business resource. With some time and creativity, your videos can open new opportunities for your small business that would make a Fortune 500 company cringe with envy. Whether it's informational videos about how to use your newest equipment or training videos for your staff, YouTube is an easy and effective way to grab the attention of your audience.

Here are ten reasons why using YouTube for small business is a must:

Take Advantage of YouTube

In 2017, YouTube reported **having 1.5 billion users every month**. Additionally, their research showed that users spend more than 1hr watching videos on their mobile devices like smartphones and tablets. YouTube is especially great for manufacturers, retailers, and service based small businesses who can use YouTube as another platform to market specialty products and techniques. Instructional and demonstrable videos are popular with potential customers doing research on a specific product. For many people it's easier and more effective for them to watch a short video and learn all they need to know than to read an article or lengthy instructions.

1.) _It's Free_

Unlike television ads or radio spots YouTube, and for the most part social media, is free. To become a visible entity on the web it takes time and effort, not money and connections like in traditional media. This medium can be leveraged so a small start up has the same potential to go viral as a more recognized brand, and that can happen very quickly with videos.

Videos and images are some of the most shared, seen, and circulated pieces of content on the internet. With a simple click users can repost something to their personal social media accounts and from there on, it spreads like wildfire.

Using YouTube for small business increases your target audience and marketing abilities with no real cost to you. YouTube is the most watched website for videos and your YouTube channel is like having a second website without the cost of hosting and upkeep.

2.) *Drive Sales*

Small businesses can use YouTube to promote their products and services to gain more valuable leads. A video on YouTube is a great referral and call back to your home website. Your video can be seen by many people, optimized, and shared through different social media tools like Facebook and Twitter. Because each video will have specific keywords or tags associated with it, it will be found by those looking for you and your products via popular search engines.

It's also interesting to note that Google, which owns YouTube, has about 70% of the search engine market. When you use Google to search, you also have the option to view "images", "maps", "videos" etc. Ever notice how every video through Google brings you to YouTube? It's a powerful medium to showcase your products and gain valuable leads that are already in your target audience.

3.) _SEO_

As I mentioned, a YouTube Channel is like having a second site and lends room for you to describe your company, the products, and the services you provide. Along with your YouTube channel, you can describe each video individually with tags to optimize them and attract the kind of viewers you actually want. Tagging your videos for SEO purposes will give you the advantage of being found in a general search.

Each SERP page provides results for videos, as well as regular articles. For instance, if you sell "baseball cards", that key term in general will have millions of results but, for video, only thousands apply.

Just like your blog articles, you want your keyword to appear in your video title, so the search engines can easily index it and your target audience can find it.

4.) _Huge Audience_

YouTube is hugely popular right now and it's grown dramatically in recent years. According to a study, 300 hours of video are uploaded to YouTube every minute! But, **only 9% of U.S. small businesses use YouTube!** There is a large, available market out there that is mostly untapped!

YouTube is a search engine like Google or Bing and is used by viewers to find useful tutorials, explanation videos, and product reviews. By creating useful videos on YouTube for small business promotion, you gain access to a much wider audience.

5.) *Product Support*

Provide your customers with useful videos on the most common problems and questions they have about a product or system. This will reduce your company's support costs and empower your customers to troubleshoot their own problems. Educational videos are a great way to bridge the gap between you and your customers, and allow them to learn going forward. A video tutorial on the proper usage of your products beats a convoluted directions page on your website any time. They can watch and pause as they're assembling as well — all with free YouTube videos.

6.) *Training*

You can use YouTube for product and training. If you have a sales force and distributors around in several states or in different countries, a short series of training videos will save you a ton of money on traveling costs and training materials. Creating and using standardized videos will ensure all your staff has access to the same information and help you communicate policy expectations. You won't lose valuable time and money on lengthy training days. You'll be able to educate everyone at the same time so they can start their jobs sooner and more efficiently. Simply upload your training videos to YouTube and grant your salespeople access. You can use these training videos for current and new employees alike to update them on any small business changes, events, or updates in the future as well.

7.) *Engagement*

You have the option to let viewers watch, comment, and share on each video. This gives your small business a unique opportunity to correspond with potential customers directly on your channel. Oftentimes, viewers will leave questions or comments about suggestions they have. You can use this feedback to give you ideas about other video topics you can create to meet your viewers' needs. Also, sharing your video via social media gives it even more exposure and chance to communicate with those on Facebook, Twitter, LinkedIn etc.

8.) *Customer Testimonials*

A video testimonial from an existing customer can go a long way. Simply having written testimonials on your website leads to the question of who actually wrote it and if it's authentic or not. Anybody can write, but with video, perspective clients can see and hear the real deal with their own eyes and ears. Being able to hear about current customers successes and thoughts will help motivate leads to become customers as well. Testimonials provide concrete proof of your small business's success and dedication to your customers and their results. The trust value and authenticity of your customer recommendations sky rocket and you'll have them forever to use for specific market strategies. You cannot put a price tag on this, it's that valuable.

9.) *Insight*

For every video you upload, YouTube offers free analytics data via the Insight feature where you can see statistics on views, demographics, community and subscribers. Most importantly, there's discovery data that shows you how people are finding your videos, including the links they followed to get there.

In addition, you can see how many views you are getting through the YouTube player page, embedded players, and mobile devices.

Just like Google Analytics, YouTube Insights provides you with useful information on how your videos are performing and what you could change to make them even more successful. You'll know if your video marketing campaigns are performing well and in what areas you should be investing in more heavily.

10.) _Fun_

Putting together a company video whether it be a holiday message or just for fun lip dub video can boost company morale. We are seeing more and more small businesses having a blast with video and their company brand. These entertaining videos convey the message that small businesses are fun to work for, easy to work with, and rewarding to do business with. Lighter side YouTube videos highlight the human nature behind the small business logo and gives a welcoming feel to future business relationships.

All of this was created in year two, to keep the stream flowing just as it did in year one year. However it didn't stop there. My mentor also told me that every great entrepreneur reads 15-25 books a month. Not any books, but those that would affect your business, your focus, your goals, even your mental and physical health. Reading not only strengthens the mind but will give you an in depth understanding of what others have done to make their business successful.

Some of my favorite people to read and listen to are Tony Robbins, Gary Vee, Les Brown, Grant Cardone, Chris Cardell, and Kevin Harrington. There are many more but over the course of 4 years, I would run out of paper listing them all.

Charlie Munger said "go to bed every night a little wiser than you were when you got up".

Many people live their lives on autopilot doing much the same thing every day and never learning anything. And the same people often wonder how it is that some people can be so successful in life and they may even think that it is because someone else has been luckier than they have. However when we look at the habits of successful people it is often the case that among other things they are voracious readers. For example:

- *Bill Gates reads one book per week.*
- *Mark Zuckerberg reads one book every two weeks.*
- *Elon musk is an avid reader.*
- *Warren Buffett spends about 80% of his day reading.*
- *Mark Cuban reads for more than three hours every day.*
- *Oprah Winfrey reads one book every month.*

If you are a wantrepreneur or an entrepreneur or a business owner there is still much to learn. Of course there is more than one way to learn what you need to know. You can learn it on your own through making mistakes in your business; sometimes this route can have fatal consequences on your business. Or you can learn from other entrepreneurs through a coach or a mentor or an advisory board or even a mastermind. This type of source learning has its place for an entrepreneur however these people are not always going to be available when you have to make vital decisions at every stage of the journey.

It is better to learn to be a good entrepreneur wherever possible in advance of challenges that may arise in running a business day-to-day. Of course some of this learning can come from other successful entrepreneurs who have done it before. But we can also learn a lot by reading books.

Reading is the best way of vicarious learningYou don't always have to make the same mistakes yourselves and you don't always have to do everything by trial and error. It is so much better to learn from other people who have done what we have done or we have not done. Reading allows us to stand on the shoulders of giants and learn from people who have triumphed against the odds and overcome huge challenges and become successful.

Obviously you have to be selective about what you read. you can't read trashy novels and expect to get any real benefit from them for your business; other than transitory entertainment. So you should make sure that you read relevant books that are educational – **books that other entrepreneurs and business owners read**. You can also read the biographies of other successful entrepreneurs to find inspiration, motivation, ideas and so much more.

Books help us in so many ways to succeed as an entrepreneur. They can be a source of inspiration, develop skills, and provide tips and business strategies. They can help us to become successful by providing the right knowledge, new ways of thinking, new insights and help us to develop the necessary skills. Reading can also influence the way that we do business through personal development and leadership skills. We can get a lot of new ideas and tips allowing us to have multiple perspectives to join the

dots and do things in a way that had never been done before.

By reading books we also develop cognitive skills which can benefit us in a multitude of ways by helping to improve our memory, develop literacy and verbal intelligence as well as increasing our strategic decision-making, boosting our brain power and reducing stress.

Not only can we learn from the successes of other entrepreneurs but we can also learn a huge amount from the failures of other entrepreneurs. It is very important to make sure that we learn about both perspectives.

Every entrepreneur, every business in every niche can benefit from the knowledge acquired through reading. Whether we are trailblazers of following in the footsteps of others there is so much we can learn from other entrepreneurs and we can always draw from the experiences of others. No business is so unique that there aren't many things that can be learned from the experience of business owners in similar and different sectors.

Reading allows us to become better entrepreneurs, making fewer mistakes in business, making more good decisions faster, and making it more likely we will have the right approach from the get go. The decisions that we make in business are based on knowledge and/or experience. Knowledge that can be derived from experiential learning of discovering what works and what doesn't or learning vicariously from someone else's experiences that they have shared in person or in a book.

When we are faced with a new and difficult situation the outcome may be unexpected. Sometimes we don't know the definite best approach to take. The more knowledge that we have either through reading or experience or data the better we will be able to make our own decisions. Obviously there are no guarantees and there are always going to be situations where even with the benefit of reading books and our own experience we will still make lots of mistakes, but we are more likely to make the right decisions more often than not.

Our problems and challenges in business are not unique. Probably every problem and challenge has been dealt with in the past by another entrepreneur as can we discover as we read more books. The answers to most problems are already available.

As an entrepreneur we have to learn and know so much – there are so many disciplines to master. Reading allows us to be smarter from the start and do things right from the beginning by learning how to from smart and successful entrepreneurs who have already dealt with the challenges we are and will face before us. It is very useful to get to understand how other entrepreneurs became successful not so that we can copy exactly what they did but to understand their processes, journey and mind-set.

Reading many books about entrepreneurs gives us a lot of perspective which allows us to realise that there is more than one way to do things. We get to understand the pros and cons of different approaches and we are able to select the best way for our businesses.

Reading books about entrepreneurs and entrepreneurialism also provides inspiration and reinforces our confidence. We may already know what we want to become and what to do but we haven't yet done anything about it. When we read we may discover confirmation of our existing knowledge and beliefs which may become a source of guidance and encouragement for us to do whatever it is we want to do.

We may feel stuck in our current position with an idea and an understanding of what it takes to set up and run a business but we are paralysed by fear. Reading may provide an additional boost to the knowledge that we have already acquired and it may help us to get unstuck by overcoming the fear. The boost of the knowledge that something worked for somebody else may also bolster our confidence to try it ourselves.

Ultimately knowledge builds like compound interest. Over time with the right approach we can combine our knowledge about business and being an entrepreneur as well as about our industry. Successful people have the self-discipline to apply and maintain this approach to business and life.

As we acquire more information through constant reading we start to connect the dots and connect information from different books and other sources. We discover things that have worked for other people in other industries and we see the opportunity to apply it in our own business. We also find that we connect information that we have acquired from books with ideas that we have had in the past allowing us to reignite something that we may have given up on in the past.

The never-ending hunger for knowledge will ultimately result in us making fewer mistakes as an entrepreneur in business. Reading books will give tips on the right way to do things.

Obviously reading doesn't totally substitute doing and we will inevitably still make mistakes along the way. If you are a wantrepreneur don't spend too long reading books it is advisable to start as soon as you can then read as you go every day.

You may be thinking that you don't have the time to be reading everyday but I would say the reason you don't have enough time to read every day is because you don't read. When we say 'no' to whatever it is that is making us too busy, we say 'yes' to reading and learning potentially better ways of running our business and life. So rather than looking at reading as something that we are saying 'yes' to, think of it as saying 'no' to a way of running our business and life in a way that does not allow us time to do other important things that will produce big future benefits.

Reading needs to be something that becomes a habit that we do every day like a ritual that fits into our daily routine. To ensure that we read every day we should set aside a block of time for reading, for example 30 minutes a day. Obviously the amount of time can be less or more than this but we need to commit to enough time to make our reading substantial enough to be worthwhile. During this time we need to find a quiet place where we are not going to be interrupted or distracted ideally without television, computers, phones, et cetera. Either first thing in the morning or last thing at night is a good time for many people to read. As Jim Rohn said "What is easy to do is easy not to do" so it is important to have a daily routine so that we keep reading consistently.

As we read the books we should also document our reading by keeping notes or writing cliff notes or a summary or creating a mind map or combinations of these. By doing this we then have something that allows us to easily refer back to important points. We can also read through our notes to quickly reinforce our recollection of the concepts learned in the book.

You will become a better and more successful entrepreneur through reading books. If you don't already read lots of quality books I implore you to do it and start right now.

Now that you are armed with even more knowledge from entrepreneurial experts who are Sharks in their perspective fields, your year two should be back on the highs of year one, but there is still a lot more ground to cover to keep you in the top of your field with your products or services.

Why you should write a book.

When my mentor my mentor/coach told me this was my next move, I literally laughed out loud. I am in the middle of the road, maybe closer to the ditch high school student, who speaks fluent Country Grammar with a lot of "slanguage." There's no way I can or would write a book. Who would read it? What could I possibly say to anyone?

I really just wanted to work on my craft and become comfortable. Not rich or wealthy, just comfortable. There was no escaping, and he was not allowing me to wiggle out of it by coming up with an excuse.

So, I started researching how to write books, who do I call. publishers etc. I even looked for ghost writers, that's how bad I didn't want to write a book.

He told me to just tell my story.

As an entrepreneur, what do you really need? What does every entrepreneur always want more of, especially for their business? ***Attention.***

I don't mean that in the narcissistic "everyone looks at me" sense.

When I say every entrepreneur wants more attention, what I mean is that attention is the key to everything else entrepreneurs want and need. It all starts with attention.

Need to sell more products or services? Start with getting people's attention, then you can show them how your product or service benefits them, leading them to make a purchase. Want to attract the best talent to your company? You have to get their attention, and show them why they want to join your company. Want to raise money? Got to get attention from VC's angels, and PE funds to pitch them.

Want media coverage? Media coverage itself is about attention, but the paradox is that you can't get any without getting the media's attention first. Want to speak at conferences or create authority for your product or company? How will anyone know they should listen if you haven't gotten their attention about what it is you have to say yet?

You see where I am going here? There are many, many ways to get attention, but writing and publishing a book is not only one the best way to get attention -- it's one of the most under-utilized by entrepreneurs.

How does a book get your attention?

A book is great for getting attention because it's a multi-purpose marketing tool with unique and special abilities to create attention that you can turn into almost anything else you want -- sales, media, word of mouth, authority. So, how does a book get your attention? There are four main ways:

1. A book gives you authority, credibility and expertise.

A lot of people like to say that "a book is the new business card." I disagree, because everyone has a business card. You can go to Office Depot and get business cards, but you can't go to Office Depot and author a book.

What I would like to say is that "a book is the new college degree." It used to be, about 40 years ago, only about 10 percent of people had college degrees. If you had one, it was a major signal of credibility and authority. It meant something. But now that everyone goes to college, it doesn't signal as much credibility.

So what is a signal of credibility and authority now -- one that's reliable and rare? Writing and publishing a book.

A book sets you up to be judged. It's really easy to skirt by and get a college degree. You can't really fake your way into writing a good book. Either you know what you're talking about or you don't. And a book shows you can commit to something and follow through. It shows you get things done, things that are hard and prestigious and require a lot of skills.

Yes, being judged is risky, but that's why you get so much credit for a good book. A book puts you in a place that most people are unwilling to go -- being judged -- and it usually requires a lot of work. It requires you to actually know something, and it requires that you show that knowledge to the world. If you write a book that's stupid, people are going to think you're stupid. But if it's good, people are going to say you're smart.

Most people are not willing to take that risk, set themselves up to be judged, and show the world what they know or don't know.

If you don't know what you're talking about, you can't just vomit out nonsense, call it a book, and get all the benefits.

You have to write a good book to gain credibility and authority, and a good book is defined by how interesting and valuable other people find it.

2. A book raises your visibility and gets media coverage.

When a media outlet wants a comment on something, who do they go to? The expert, right? And how do they know someone is an expert? Because they wrote the book. Experts write books. Commentators write blog posts.

Once you have a book, media coverage is 10 times easier to get. It's not just the media either. "Has a new book" is a standard, and often required, box to tick for the gatekeepers who control access to areas you most want to enter -- lecture halls, television studios, boardrooms, media pages, special events, people's minds.

Charlie Rose doesn't say "My next guest has just posted a cat video."

How many people in your field have you seen get a lot of attention simply because they wrote a book? Even if you knew more than them, they got the attention that you didn't, only because of the book. If you want visibility in your field and media coverage, being an authority and expert is key to this, and the way you do that is to write a book.

3. A book helps people find you.

Google is the top ranked internet search engine, followed by YouTube. Do you know who is in third place? Amazon. And even more relevant to entrepreneurs, Amazon is the No. 1 search engine when looking for products and services, with 44 percent of searches for products and services starting there.

This goes beyond just attention. An ad can get attention, but no one goes searching for ads to make a decision about buying a product or a service. When people look for buying information, they turn to experts or authorities. And where's the first place they think about to find information from an expert? Same as the media. They look at the person who literally "wrote the book" on the topic.

Having a great book brings people to you, lets people know exactly who you are, and shows them how you can help them. It's the best marketing tool you could ever use to not just build your brand, but actually attract clients.

Here's a perfect example. When I began to write my first book, N.E.X.T. -Nobody Ever eXpected This, I was looking for people who have written books on how to write a book. In that search it led me to The Words Lady, Vickie Gould.

Being a successful multiple best selling author on Amazon, in my eyes, she was an expert. At that she was offering an online course in How to write your best seller in 30 days. This was right up my alley.

To make a long story short, it was because of her books that I took her course, hence my book rose to #5 Hot New Sellers on Amazon.

And it all came about because he had told me I should write a book.

4. A book helps people talk about you.

There is no better marketing than word of mouth. When someone you trust tells you to use something, you listen, and you use it. Anything that helps other people talk about you and your business is the best marketing tool possible. A book enables word of mouth better than almost anything else.

This is because a book puts your story into people's mouths -- in your words. When people talk about you, they're literally just saying what you want them to say. A good book causes people to repeat your terms, phrases and ideas to other people.

We use this idea to help authors position and frame their books. Let's say, "Imagine someone at a cocktail party who read your book, talking to someone else in your potential audience. What would they say? Imagine what you want them to say to the other."

Once you understand that -- once you can picture that conversation naturally happening between two people -- you can almost construct the positioning and narrative of your book from that conversation.

This is exactly what Vickie had done for me. Whenever I meet people who want to write a book, I tell them how I solved the problem, and I tell them the things I learned from her book and online course. Even if I don't directly refer to them, they end up reaching out to Vickie's facebook page.

If you can write a book that is valuable to people, they will want to talk about your book to someone else who has that problem. Why? Because it makes them look good. That's how word of mouth works. I look good to people when I tell them about Vickie's book, because it's a great book, and it makes me look good to provide valuable knowledge to other people.

Books turn attention into money.

Attention is great, but most entrepreneurs don't just want attention and nothing else. The reason entrepreneurs want attention is because they can turn it into money. Remember what I said earlier, that a book is a multi-purpose marketing tool that creates attention that you can turn into almost anything else you want? I'm going to make this concept even more simple: Book = Attention = Money.

There are so many ways for entrepreneurs to leverage the attention from a book into money. I'll run through the most common ways to do this, with examples for each:

1. A book can launch consulting and

coaching companies.

At Strategic Target Marketing, Once they reach a certain level of success -- they can't really go much higher without a book. In fact, it is often the book that takes them from small time with a few clients to building an actual business.

You might be thinking something like, "But if I write a book talking about what I know, why will people hire me to be a consultant for them?"

Well, like I said, the book is how people find you. A great example of this is Kevin Harrington. In only a few years, he went from the unknown creator and Father of Infomercials, to such a well-respected investor and original shark on the hit TV show "Shark Tank." He speaks to such mega conference groups as Grant Cardone's 10X. How'd he do that? Well, a lot of hard work of course, but he attributes most of success to his multiple best selling books, and how they really put him on the map.

And I already talked about how I found Vickie -- her book made me want to learn more. Most of what she teaches on a day-to-day basis is in her book.

Russeell Brunson book doubled the size of his business. When he wrote his first book on funnel hacking, every social media influencer wanted to interview him, and the book led to clients seeing him in totally different ways. His book positioned him as an expert in a hot new field. He put a ton of what he knew in his book, and it was the only reason he got hired by major entrepreneurs who wanted to expand their business on social media. They wanted to know what he knew.

That's the point. People who hire consultants and coaches are hiring them to teach them and their team and to implement their knowledge. They're often not looking to learn the knowledge in the book. The book is how you show them that they should hire you.

2. A book can sell a physical product.

Another very profitable way to monetize a book is by using it to promote a physical product. Go search on Amazon under books for "lose weight" or "eat paleo." You'll see thousands of books, and a lot of them are essentially buyer's guides for physical products, like supplements, food companies or one-off products.

Take Mark Sisson for example, who started Primal Blueprint. He's published nearly a dozen books about his version of the paleo diet. They're great books. He sells them on Amazon and even gives many of them away on his site. Sisson also has a complete line of Primal Blueprint supplements and food that people can buy. They don't have to buy them, but it's there, easy to do, and the books and products dovetail perfectly.

Think about it. Would you respond to an ad about supplements? Probably not. But what about a book that teaches you what supplements to take, when and why? If you trust the book, you'll trust the supplement recommendations. Because Sisson has great books -- and a great site -- on eating that you trust, you automatically give his supplement recommendations more credibility, and buy his brand.

3. A book can sell a software product.

A book is a great way for a company to sell software, especially SaaS software. The best example is HubSpot. That company invented inbound marketing, and how did they promote it? Among other things, they wrote a book called Inbound Marketing.

The book doesn't even pitch HubSpot very much. It is essentially a massive advertisement for their method of marketing, and guess what? Using their software is the easiest way to actually do inbound marketing, so not only does the book provide real value to the reader, it ends up converting a lot of readers to customers.

4. A book can sell a video course/information product.

Using your book as a marketing tool and lead generation for a video course is such a good way to make money from a book. Basically, if your book teaches something for which there is a high ROI for the reader, you can create an advanced version that is delivered as a video course -- and charge much more money for it.

People will not pay more than about $25 for a book, but they will often pay $500 or more for a video course of the exact same material. This actually is rational, because many people learn more easily from video and audio than they do from books. Whether it's rational or not doesn't matter. What matters is that writing a book and using it to sell similar material as a video course is a great way to make money.

Jeremy McGilvrey wrote a book called Instagram Secrets. It's about how to use Instagram to drive sales, drive traffic, grow your following, and generate predictable profits for your company. The book, while very good, ends up driving many people to his advanced video course.

5. A book can recruit employees to work for your company.

This is overlooked, but for entrepreneurs and C-level executives alike, there is almost no better way to get great people to work with you than by laying your vision for your company out in a book.

The best example of this is Zappos. Not only did Tony Shieh write his own book, but he also wrote a different book about Zappos culture -- that they give away on their site as a way to get people to come work for them. To this day, the book is still the main lead generation for recruiting at Zappos.

6. A book can promote "done for you" services.

Strategic Target Marketing is a great example. I developed an innovative way to turn your ideas, products and services into a social media campaign ad -- something many are doing, very few are doing and are successful -- then I proceeded to explain the entire process. I mean literally, the whole process, including the templates I use with other entrepreneurs.

Why the hell would I do that? It's the same logic you've heard me say over and over again. My program, Strategic Target Marketing, shows potential business owners and entrepreneurs my process so they can understand it and see how great it is. Saying the process is great is totally different than proving it in detail.

I've had so many clients who were skeptical, see the results I post on social media, or my YouTube channel, and were like, "This is a genius, I'm going to do it myself." Then, even though they loved the process, many realized their time was too valuable, so they just came back to me as full clients.

To the people who can't afford STM, no problem. Go do it yourself. I'm not losing a client by telling them how to do it themselves. In fact, the more people who use my method, the better. They'll talk about STM and my process, creating word of mouth advertising.

7. A book can help draw clients to you.

Especially if you sell B2B services, like marketing or advertising, a book is a huge asset in drawing and closing clients. Just ask Mitch Joel. He started and runs Mirum Digital Agency, which does a ton of business almost exclusively with big brands and companies. When he walks in a room to pitch a CMO, he can bring copies of his books with him to reinforce all the points he's making. It's 10 times better than any brochures or anything else he could leave.

8. A book can launch and promote paid community/mastermind groups.

There's so many people who have paid Masterminds, and so many of their clients find out about them and want to join their group because they've written books that show everyone how much they know.

A great example is Jayson Gaignard. He has a group called Mastermind Talks, and a book called Mastermind Dinners. His book explains exactly how he built and runs his mastermind group and how he is such a successful networker and connector. This, in turn, ends up driving a lot of sign-ups for his group, which is a paid community and meet-up group.

Another example is James Maskell. He runs the Evolution of Medicine Summit and mastermind group, where tens of thousands of health professionals meet and discuss topics.

9. A book can launch workshops and group teaching.

Many consultants and speakers also do what is called group workshops. Business will bring you in to teach your method to their employees and train them over a day or a series of days. It's really easy to get relatively larger businesses to pay you to come in to teach a one-day workshop to their employees about what you know. Why? Because so few people take the time to read all the way through a book.

If you read books, you are way ahead of the curve, but I know, as most employers know, if they pass a book out, their employees aren't going to read it. If they get the person who wrote the book to come in and give a speech, and to answer questions for a day, they can really teach the staff.

A great example is Mona Patel, who wrote the book Reframe. She now does workshops based on applying the book that routinely sells out. Both things reinforce each other. The book leads people to the workshop, and she sells copies of her book to people who come to the workshop.

I've done the exact same thing with my company Premier Leather Crafters. The only difference, I reached out to one of my supplies and just asked them could I put on a workshop? To my surprise the GM is a follower to one of my social media pages as well as my YouTube channel.

I worked a deal where the student crafters would pay me a fee for the class and I in turn would buy the supplies needed from my supplier.

My very first class teaching how to make leather sandals brought four students at $100 each. Not too bad for a 4 hour class in a free venue.

I used my book, YouTube, and social media to establish I am credible. And it didn't hurt that the GM is a follower/subscriber.

10. A book can help you raise money.

I would not recommend this for companies in the seed stage, but later stage companies that have traction can absolutely get a lot of results from a book.

A lot of entrepreneur's write Medium posts to raise money. That's fine, but someone with a good book is way better. Shane Mac used this strategy to raise money for his first startup. His book was a deeply honest and engaging story about how he ran his company, and he would send it to VC's before pitches. (It's also really helped him recruit talent to his new company Assist).

One of the iconic examples is the book The Promise Of A Pencil. Though this is a charity and not a startup, the principle is exactly the same. Adam Braun used the book to generate a ton of attention and money poured into his charity.

The point is -- use the book as the pitch deck in advance. It tells your story so well, that you get VC's coming to you asking to put money in.

11. A book can get you speaking appearances.

One of the major ways to get attention and make money from a book is using it to become a speaker. A book is a business card for a speaker. It's kind of a necessity. A book is the way people know for sure you are qualified to speak to their group on your topic.

A great example of this was after my first book hit Hot New Seller on Amazon. I immediately started looking for small groups of entrepreneurs that:

1. **Needed a boost in sales**
2. **Wanted more customers and clients**
3. **Were at the wits in on scaling**
4. **Didn't have a clue on how to tweak the analytics on social media to drive sales and traffic to their business**

I have not joined the ranks of Gary Vee, Tony Robbins, Les Brown or Grant Cardone, but I was able to replace a 9-5 monthly income with speaking events.
Start small with high schools, junior colleges, and universities. Your local Chamber of Commerce put on monthly events for

their members, which you can pull double duty and get some much networking done.

12. A book can promote a conference.

Books are a very underexploited marketing avenue for conferences. I've been working with my entire team with STM, Book Robertt D Muhammad, and Premier Leather Crafters on developing and sponsoring mini seminars and workshops combine in a 2 day weekend . It pairs business owners in that space with the leather crafters and thought leaders. What we do is record the entire conference and turn it into a book. The conference I host does two things.

- *I'll send copies of the book to other crafters, business owners or potential entrepreneurs*

- *I'll include a copy of the book when I mail out the physical applications for each conference. It's tripled my re-up rate.*

By spending $5 to mail a nice book to past participants, I get them to spend $249+ on a conference that is more than 6 months away. Pretty good deal.

13. A book can save you taxes through write-offs.

This is a great way to make money that way too few business owners use. If you are using your book as a legitimate marketing tool to promote a business, the costs of production are 100 percent deductible. That means everything you spend money creating the book can be deducted. The book cover, the layout, the printing costs, the proofreading, professional services, the books you buy to teach you how to write your book, the software you buy to help you write the book. I could go on and on.

It's all 100 percent deductible as a business marketing expense. Just like you can deduct what you spend on Facebook ads and website designers, a book falls into the same category.

Here's the rub with that -- your time is not deductible. If you spend 500 hours at a computer typing away, you are totally out of luck. You cannot deduct the opportunity cost of your time from your taxes, even though that 500 hours is stopping you from making money doing other things.

If you are a coach, and people pay you $200 an hour for coaching, spending 500 hours writing a book -- instead of coaching -- costs you $100,000 in forgone income. You absolutely cannot deduct that, even though it is a very real cost to you. But if you hire someone to help you write your book, then you absolutely can deduct that cost.

This is another reason why so many people use our service, even if they can write the book themselves. If they pay us $20,000 to help them author their book, not only is that cost fully deductible, but they save hundreds, oftentimes thousands, of hours. That time can be spent working in their business, doing what they do best.

When you figure in the tax savings plus the time savings, it's almost like getting the book for free for most of our authors -- and that is before they get any of the attention and ROI from the book.

NOTE -- I am talking about tax laws in America. Though this is what many tax lawyers have told me, you should never take legal advice from someone on the internet who does not know the laws of your specific jurisdiction.

Important! Do not focus on book sales.

I'm going to tell you something counterintuitive. Entrepreneurs should not focus on making money directly from book sales. Why? Because this is a fact of the book publishing business -- it's nearly impossible to sell a lot of copies of a book, at least enough to make it worth your time as a business owner.

Last year, there were more than 300,000 new books published in America. BookScan, the company that measures all book sales, says that only about 200 books per year sell 100,000 copies. The number of books that reached 1 million sold last year is even fewer, probably close to 10, and almost all of those were novels. And virtually no book does more than that. The list of books that have sold 10 million copies in history is so small there's a Wikipedia page about them.

What's even worse is that you can't charge enough for books to generate good revenue from them. The highest you can charge is about $25, give or take. The greatest book ever written, if it costs more than that, won't get bought. People have a low limit on their perceived value for books.

There is only one group of people who must focus on how many copies they sell -- that's professional writers. And they can worry about sales numbers because that's the only way they make money! They don't have anything else to sell but their book. But this is not true for an entrepreneur.

Focusing on direct sales creates bad decisions for entrepreneurs, because they try to write a broad book in an attempt to speak to a large audience, instead of focusing on a niche that would get the best results for their business.

If you look at your book as a marketing tool for driving attention to something that does make money, then everything changes. Your book is essentially a different form of paid marketing, that looks and acts in its own unique ways.

If you don't believe me, then at least listen to James Altucher.

"Every entrepreneur should self-publish a book, because having a book is the new business card. If you want to stand out, you need to show your expertise. Publishing a book is not just putting your thoughts on a blog post. It's an event. It shows your best curated thoughts and it shows customers, clients, investors, friends and lovers what the most important things on your mind are right now."

For most entrepreneurs, a book is the very best multi-purpose marketing they can have. The only thing left is to start the process.

Our busy lives limit the time we can spend with a book; so, why not turn to the alternative?

A lot has been written about how many millionaires and billionaires read, and the numbers are pretty daunting. From Warren Buffet reading 500 pages a day to Mark Zuckerberg's 2015 book-reading pledge to Bill Gates's 50-books-a-year habit, the rich and famous read voraciously.

Now, I'm a reader myself and there are few things I love more than to journey into the mind of another successful entrepreneur. I know how important it is for professionals to continue learning, to develop their skills and talents in a competitive marketplace.

But no matter how much I may want to read every book on this year's "Best Seller" lists, my life just isn't set up to spend hours every day curled up with the most recent cool title. And the same probably holds true for most entrepreneurs and small business owners.

That's why I rely on podcasts, and why you should too.

So, why podcasts?

For these reasons, podcasts have moved to the very top of my list of the best life hacks of recent years. Whenever and wherever I have my phone, earbuds and a little time, I listen to programs that can broaden my perspective and grow my understanding of my job, my life and the world. Podcasts are entertainment and education rolled into one and tailor-made for my multi-tasking life.

Podcasts are also evolving; they've come a long way since their humble beginnings in 2003. Technological advances and the ubiquity of broadband connections have enabled mobile apps to easily integrate players and stream podcasts almost anywhere.

With smartphones ranked as the top medium for podcast consumption, 44 percent of Americans, or approximately 143 million people, have now listened to at least one podcast, according to Edison Research. Here are the top four reasons why you should join them.

1. *To your brain, listening is the same as reading.*

Like many people, you may feel that listening is somehow "cheating," when compared to reading. This is an especially common concern among people who listen to audiobooks: that, somehow, you're getting too much reward for too little effort. But research reported by Sage Publications shows there's no difference in comprehension between listening and reading content. You aren't cheating -- you're just adding to your store of knowledge and understanding through a different medium.

2. *You can probably find the information you need.*

Regardless of the topic you're hoping to learn more about, it seems there's now a podcast for that. In fact, with 550,00 active podcasts on Apple's app alone, and over 18.5 million episodes available, you'd be hard pressed not to find what you're looking for.

3. *Multi-tasking much?*

The ability to listen to high-quality content no matter where you are or what you're doing is a big reason for the growth of podcasting over the past 15 years. And this medium is especially attractive for entrepreneurs, who are busy building a company, often with their own two hands.

Not only can you listen during your commute, while waiting in line or on a plane, but you can also listen while you're doing all those activities of daily living that eat up so much time, from laundry to home maintenance and repairs. And 11 percent of podcast listeners turn on programs while they're working, which can be great for entrepreneurs taking care of their routine business tasks.

4. The quality of the experience can be extraordinary.

Long before human beings first carved figures on cave walls, people were gathering together to share stories that taught, inspired and entertained. We seem to be wired to absorb what we hear, so when we listen to a podcast, we tend to listen intently. We don't skim or scan the way we might do with a news article or a blog post. We create images in our minds of the scenes being described. We connect to the story, and we learn.

Of course, listening to podcasts isn't going to instantly catapult you into the ranks of the ultra-successful: people like Warren Buffet, Steve Jobs et al. They had to do a lot of work to translate all their reading into the bottom line. But podcasts will definitely put you in the company of the more-successful: 51 percent of monthly podcast listeners have incomes of

$75,000 and over, as compared to only 38 percent of the general population, according to The Podcast Consumer 2018 report.

Starting a podcast is a Gold Mine

Since the dawn of digital there has been a ton of talk about what your company should be doing for digital marketing. Whether it is paid search, social media or blogging, there is no shortage of ideas and advice. However, one of the undeniable forces drawing businesses and their customers closer together is the ability to weave a better story.

Content marketing is a great way for brands to tell their story, and I would argue that one of the best vehicles for content marketing today has to be the podcast. Indeed, podcasts like Serial have found a way to captivate an audience of hundreds of thousands, and create a loyal following. The buzz around that particular podcast has primed the medium for take off.

Besides uncovering interesting and relevant information chosen by the person, podcasts are an easily consumable content format, and it doesn't require a person's undivided attention like video or text-based content does.

Here are five reasons why you should start exploring the benefits of podcasting for your business, now:

1. You can become more intimate with your audience.

When there are a zillion more brands and businesses vying for audience attention in the online space, it's evident that the plain old tricks of content marketing may not keep working for your business. You've got to be different. By allowing you to talk to your audience directly, in your own voice, podcasts help you connect with your audience on a deeper and more personal level.

2. You have the whole playground for yourself. Well, almost.

Despite the benefits and the relative ease of podcasting, few businesses are actually doing it. Including podcasts in your content-marketing strategy can give you the leverage that helps you stay ahead of your competitors.

Take cues from the experts who are doing it right. I'll point you to some very credible voices doing a great job of podcasting: Michael Stelzner, Pat Flynn, Jay Baer, Srinivas Rao, and of course you should give Serial a listen. This gang can help you start your podcasting venture on the right foot and Serial will show you a prime example of what is working for this medium.

3. There are many possibilities with podcasting.

If you think that podcasts are for one-way communication with your audience, you might be mistaken. You can share your ideas with your audience in so many different ways with podcasts. You can review products and services. You can invite an expert or thought leader to be a guest on your "show." You can interview experts, and even consumers. Podcasting is a great way to put forth the views of people your audience is most likely to trust -- experts, and their peers.

4. You can distribute podcasts through multiple channels.

While the most common thing to do is to broadcast your podcasts on your website or blog, you can spread their reach across the global audience through services like iTunes, Stitcher and SoundCloud. You can also use social channels to share your podcasts with your audience.

5. Podcasts connect employees to their organization.

Podcasts not only brings your brand closer to your audience but also gives you a scope to connect with your own employees. You can use podcasts for training your employees, making announcements and applauding them for their good work. Once you earn their trust and satisfaction with your brand, they will be among the first ones in line to buy your products or tout your services.

There's nothing stopping you. Go get your recorder and start podcasting. I'm sure it will be one of the smartest decisions you'll ever make for your small business.

How to get more customers.

There's only one way to achieve that financial freedom and that is the acquisition of customers. Getting customers is the biggest problem in business. It's also the area that business owners struggle with the most. This happens more often with businesses who have a product, milder cases with service businesses but it can still happen. Business Plateau is leveling off, this is where scaling comes in.

We spend so much time perfecting our product or service, only to realise that this means nothing if we don't somehow become amazing at getting customers. Once you realise that the business you are really in is the "getting customers business, and you decide to get very good at it, you are virtually guaranteed financial freedom.

Accomplishing this goal is by focusing on the unconverted leads. An unconverted lead is somebody who has phoned, emailed or come into your establishment or made some kind of contact with you and expressed an interest in what you have to offer, but they have not followed through and bought, for whatever reason.

The biggest mistake business owners make is thinking that because someone didn't buy today, this week, this month they're never going to buy from you. That's not true.

Think of it this way, are you an impulse shopper? If that answer is no then most likely your customers are the same way. Eventually, just like you, they will come around, but you have to sweeten the pot, and the way you do that is through gift certificates, discount codes/coupons, or giveaways.

I have done the very same thing in my company. I like to do giveaways and ad campaigns on social media. I like to call the Enticement Gifts, a leather key fob, or a leather id bracelet. Something small but it showcases my craftsmanship. It is my belief that once a future potential client/customer physically holds one of my pieces, it would trigger them to either look at my website more closely or buy something right then.

The form of contact is going to vary slightly depending on the business you're in, but the principle is always the same. On average, your customers are going to need an email, another email, maybe a phone call, maybe another email, maybe something in a post, maybe a face-to-face meeting if it's appropriate for you, maybe another email or two, and only then do they become a customer.

You absolutely need to do multiple follow-ups. If somebody comes within a mile of your business, you want to have a system in place for this, whether it be email, direct mail, telephone calls, or other forms of good marketing.

Referrals bring in customers.

There are 3 primary ways to get referrals.

1.) through your existing customers.

2.) You can ask your supplier to refer you to customers. There are some more advanced things around referrals, that for some reason, people tend to overlook supplier referrals. Establish a good relationship with your suppliers, if you haven't already, ask the question, and get the contact details of all those untapped customers.

3.) Referral Campaigns People generally accept that they should have marketing campaigns in their business, meaning you promote a specific product or service, and you have a marketing campaign that consists of things you swend through the mail, emails, a website, and a specific web page set up for it.

It is important that you understand you need a marketing campaign just for referrals. Referral customers are great for two reasons, they are free.

Second, they are better customers.

This also can open up even more cash flow streams because through your supplier referrals or just your suppliers workshops and seminars can be put on.

A year ago, I was working on my supplier referrals and it led to me putting on a workshop at one of my suppliers in Birmingham, Al. It was a simple deal that worked for both of us. Those signing up where to buy their supplies from my supplier and I had a free location and the money from the fees.

The best weapon for you to have in your arsenal, as an entrepreneur, is having an all around knowledge of the art and science of getting customers. Sure, anyone can run off a list of how-tos, however if you really want to become superb at getting customers, you really must understand and be able to practise the art of it.

Your ability to sell effectively is as important to your ability to get customers as anything else, and it always will be. A lot of businesses regardless of product or service go into business to sell. They don't think, after quitting their jobs, they want to become salesman all day everyday. I'm sure you've realised by now, this is nowhere near enough to be successful. Everything in your business success boils down to two things. Sales and marketing.

Whether you're growing a huge company or a business in a small back bedroom, you are an entrepreneur. As an entrepreneur you have to become **GREAT** at selling.

There are many ways to improve your sales skills but you need to understand the fundamental importance of sales as part of the customers attraction and acquisition strategy within your business.

One of the biggest questions you'll need to answer as you formulate plans to start your business is where you will locate it. Will you work from home or set up an office, storefront or other commercial space? In some cases, you'll have no choice, as the needs of your business or zoning laws may decide for you. But very often, the decision will be yours. If you're trying to decide whether to start a home-based business vs. brick and mortar business, each option has pluses and minuses, so here are some things to consider.

The Benefits of a Home-Based Business

On the plus side: The commute is nonexistent. On those cold, snowy mornings, the only digging out you'll do is unearthing a clean coffee cup from the dishwasher. You'll have no commuting-related expenses, whether by automobile or mass transit. No gas, no tolls, no bus or train tickets. No morning or evening traffic jams.

You can multitask. Since you're home, you can make productive use of your forced downtime by taking care of some domestic chores at the same time. While you're on hold with a client, you can sort the laundry or take something out of the freezer to defrost for dinner. That load of wash can run while you're updating your website. Dinner can cook as you work on sales projections. Many small odds and ends that would normally pile up for evenings and weekends can now be accomplished during your workweek.

You have more control over your schedule. If you're a morning person, you can get up at 5 AM and start your workday. Clean out your email inbox, start on that next pitch and read today's trade paper before you need to wake your kids up and get them off to school. Prefer evenings? When the family's in bed and the house is quiet is the perfect time to work on your next client presentation. It's difficult to keep such flexible hours when you're at the mercy of an office complex. Should you have a half hour free, you can actually use that time to work instead of *getting* to work.

You don't have to pay rent. Other than possibly upgrading your internet service to allow for more speed, working from home won't cost you any more than your current living expenses. Find an unused corner in the basement, work out of your guest room, or clear off your dining room table. Your apartment rent or mortgage payment won't change, and you're utilizing the space you have anyway to actually make money.

There are tax benefits. You'll want to familiarize yourself with the laws and regulations, but if you qualify, you can deduct part of your home's expenses against your business income. These may include a portion of your mortgage interest, property taxes, utilities and home maintenance.

The Internal Revenue Service is your best source for the rules concerning home office deductions. The startup cost is lower. Working out of your home significantly cuts the amount of money you will need to get started, even if you don't plan to keep the business there for long. Without the expense and commitment of signing a lease, buying furniture, and installing a commercial phone system, computers and other office equipment, you can jump right in and get going with your plans. Use your cell phone for a while, visit the library for a copier or printer if you don't have one, and make do with your home computer for now. If and when the business grows, you can then decide if you'd like to keep it at home or move out.

There is no office politics. And no dress code! It's true, you really *can* work in your pajamas if you want to (although you might feel more productive if you get dressed). Depending on whether you have any employees working with you at home, no one knows what you're wearing and no one cares. Similarly, there's no office pecking order and no gamesmanship from other workers.

You are a role model. Of course, this is true whether you dutifully pack your attaché case and leave home for an office every day or work out of your house, but if you have children, your commitment and hard work is a terrific example and can be a powerful influence on how they dedicate themselves in their own lives. When you work from home, they actually get to see you at work, and understand the discipline, focus, and effort involved. This can reap benefits for your family far beyond the paycheck you earn.

The Negatives of a Home-Based Business

Of course, there are some potential downsides to working at home, as well. It can be lonely. Without the camaraderie of coworkers, you can occasionally feel isolated and alone. Now, some of us may work best with fewer distractions, but even then, from time to time we like to share a joke around the water cooler or bounce an idea off a colleague. You may want to schedule socialization time during your work day. You can work from the local coffee shop for a couple of hours, plan to attend a monthly networking meeting, or meet a client face-to face. Just don't spend every moment at home by yourself.

You're in charge. While being accountable only to yourself is a wonderful thing, it also requires great dedication, motivation and self-discipline. If you are the type of worker who thrives on feedback and the energy of others, working at home can be quite challenging. You'll also need to be able to say no to the distractions of your surroundings, like the big-screen TV in the den or the pool in the backyard. It's tougher to get started and easier to procrastinate when working at home. Boundaries can be overstepped. Similarly, your family will need to respect your boundaries, and the lines can sometimes blur. It may look like you're not working even when you are. It may be easier for family and friends to take you less seriously when you work from home, so you need to be vigilant about maintaining a proper separation and level of professionalism, and teach everyone to respect your time and space.

Your clients may need convincing. Like it or not, there is something about an office that says "professional." Unless you've got a separate entrance and a truly dedicated office space, home-based businesses don't lend themselves especially well toward visits from current or potential customers, and meeting at the local diner isn't always the best solution. Your neighbors might not appreciate the traffic, either. Depending on what type of business you've got, zoning laws may actually prohibit you from running it out of your home. Make sure you're up on all the local rules and regulations. There is no "walk-in" traffic. Having a physical location can sometimes result in bonus business just because customers can see you and decide to try your product or service. Your networking opportunities will also be reduced, simply because you're not physically present with other people.

It's not cost-free. Even though you might be saving on rent, you will need to heat or cool your home office space for the day, which means running the heat or air conditioner when you otherwise might not. You will also need the office supplies and equipment to carry out the business at hand. Your computer will need to be able to run whatever software you might require, and you'll likely want a separate business landline installed or possibly another cell phone to handle business calls. Expansion is limited. If your goal is to stay a sole practitioner, this is not a problem. But if success for your business requires additional employees, you will likely outgrow the space you have at home. Moreover, do you even *want* employees in your home? You sacrifice a great deal of privacy and personal space when you allow others to work with you, especially if you don't have dedicated space in your home.   You can't leave. Well, yes, you can walk out of the room and shut the door, but your office is always THERE. Will you be able to get the mental space you need knowing there's a work issue just down the hall, or will you feel compelled to tackle it even when you're supposed to be "off"?

Advantages of a Brick and Mortar Business

Looking over the lists of pros and cons of working at home, it's easy to translate them into an understanding of the benefits and negatives of having a brick and mortar space.

Room to Grow. You can get more and larger space than you likely have available at home, so when you need to expand, you can.

Professional Front.

Some people believe a commercially-based business presents a more credible and professional face. Dedicated Work Space. You have a ready-made space to meet with clients. Boundaries. Your work time and space is separate and distinct from your family life and your living space.

Room for Employees.

Do you need to hire employees? Go right ahead. There are fewer privacy concerns with having employees. Social Energy. You will have more people around to fuel your creativity, more of those "happy accidents" that sometimes happen just from talking with and being around others. Single Tasking. You can leave most of your home concerns at home. No pressure to clean the bathrooms or defrost the freezer while you're at work.

Disadvantages of a Brick and Mortar Business

Expense. It can be costly to pay rent, buy office furniture, equipment, supplies, and maintain insurance. Commuting. You will have to commute and pay whatever costs may be associated with that. No Home-Office Tax Break. You will lose the home-office deduction if you currently qualify. Wardrobe Budget. You may need to spend more on office-appropriate clothing.

Inconvenience. Unless you take time off, you will not be at home for a sick child, repair appointment or package delivery.

Home-Based AND Brick and Mortar

As you can see, there are pros and cons to working from home *and* having a brick and mortar presence. Keep exploring where setting up your office will work best. Only you can decide which work environment is most beneficial to your business, and where your job and life satisfaction will be the highest.

Keep in mind there are no absolutes. You may be primarily based out of your home but lease space in a shared office environment a few days out of the month. You might take commercial space and telecommute one or two days a week. For many, a blend of the two works best. This past April, Yahoo's CEO Marissa Mayer said, "People are more productive when they're alone"¦(but) more collaborative and innovative when they're together. Some of the best ideas come from pulling two different ideas together." Perhaps this piece of advice applies to where you choose to work, as well.

Scaling your business

So you've made the decision to grow your business – congratulations! Now get ready for the next challenge: how to scale your business for growth. Even if you manage to sell like crazy, you'll soon have another problem: you have to be able to deliver to all those new customers.

Scalability is about capacity and capability. Does your business have the capacity to grow? Will your business systems, infrastructure and team be able to accommodate growth?

If growth causes your company to stumble because of confusion, orders falling through the cracks, insufficient staff, miscommunication, not enough manufacturing or delivery capacity – you're going to have unhappy customers. The manual processes that were fine when you were small but now won't let you move fast enough. You'll either be putting out fires or desperately trying to keep your head above water. All of which is stressful.

Scaling a business means setting the stage to enable and support growth in your company. It means having the ability to grow without being hampered. It requires planning, some funding and the right systems, staff, processes, technology and partners.

Here are five critical steps to scaling your business:

Evaluate and Plan

Take a hard look inside your business to see if you are ready for growth. You can't know what to do differently unless you take stock of where your business stands today.

Strategize what you need to do to increase sales. Then assume your orders doubled or tripled overnight. Does your organization have the people and systems to handle those new orders, without failing or getting a big black eye? This is where a good plan is essential.

The best planning in my view starts with a detailed sales growth forecast, broken down by number of new customers, orders and revenue you want to generate. Include a spreadsheet that breaks the numbers down by month. The more specific you are, the more realistic your sales acquisition plan can be. Then do a similar expense forecast, based on adding technology, people, infrastructure and systems to handle all those new sales orders. Look at every item on your current P&L to see how it might be impacted. Expenses will go up -- you have to anticipate where and how. Again, include an expense spreadsheet that breaks down expenses needed to meet your sales forecast.

Try to think of everything. You'll need to do some hard thinking and research to come up with proper cost estimates, but doing so will make your plan better.

Find the Money

Scaling a business doesn't come free. Your growth plan may call for hiring staff, deploying new technology, adding equipment and facilities, and creating reporting systems to measure and manage results. How will you find the money to invest for growth? I'm a huge proponent of bootstrapping, but it typically takes years to grow through bootstrapping alone. There are also small business contests with cash prizes such as the FedEx Small Business Grant Contest which starts taking entries Feb. 21, 2017. If you have a great story to tell about your business and could use a $25,000 grant and $7,500 in FedEx Office® print and business services to boost your business, this is an amazing opportunity. It's also helpful to identify potential bank funds to accelerate growth such as a loan or a line of credit to draw on – start with how much you'll need. And get started applying.

Secure the Sales

Scaling your business obviously assumes you will sell more. Do you have the sales structure in place to generate more sales? Look at sales from end to end. Do you have:

- **A sufficient lead flow to generate the desired number of leads?**
- **Marketing systems to track and manage leads?**
- **Enough sales representatives to follow up and close leads?**

- A robust system to manage sales orders?
- A billing system and a receivables function to follow up to ensure invoices are collected timely?

Invest in Technology

Technology makes it easier and less expensive to scale a business. You can gain huge economies of scale and more throughput, with less labor, if you invest wisely in technology.

- *Automation can help you run your business at a lower cost and more efficiently by minimizing manual work.*
- *Systems integration is a prime area for improvement in most businesses. Companies today don't run off of a single*

system -- they may have a dozen or more systems. If those systems don't work together, they create silos, which in turn multiply communication and management problems as your company grows.

Now's a good time to evaluate new products on the market that save time and money, yet accommodate much higher volumes in every part of your business. Look at CRM, marketing automation, sales management, inventory, manufacturing, accounting, HR, shipping and other technology systems.

Evaluate not only software, but also networks and hardware such as servers, computers, printers and telephony equipment.

<u>Find Staff or Strategically Outsource</u>

Last but certainly not least, are the hands needed to carry out the work. Technology gives huge leverage, but at the end of the day you still need people.

- ***Do you have enough customer service staff? Look at industry benchmarks to determine a rule of thumb for how many customers one service rep can be expected to handle.***
- ***What about the people who are responsible for your manufacturing, inventory and delivery of product or services? How many are typical for your industry per customer, and how many will you need?***
- ***How do you find qualified help quickly? Recruiting and hiring systems are important, as are benefits and payroll.***
- ***Don't forget management. The importance of a management bench grows as your business grows. You won't be able to oversee everything.***

Sometimes the answer is to **_outsource or look to partners,_** rather than hiring internally.

Scaling requires that you make tough choices. What functions can and should you perform -- or not perform -- internally?

Third parties may have the staff and investment in systems that enable them to be much more efficient in handling a function than your company. Trying to replicate that function internally may take too much time or money. Instead, **_find a reliable partner to outsource, thus positioning your business to scale better, faster and cheaper._**

These are five factors to consider in scaling a business.

Online Sales

Even though the notion of retailing online is not new, many retailers still do not operate an e-commerce website. There are many online retailing advantages and key benefits that retailers could harness by operating successful online retail stores.

There are some key benefits that are hard to ignore, when it comes to online retailing. Selling online is just very efficient, has lower barriers to entry, streamlined communication, improved customer service, and so much more.

Start-up businesses and smaller companies especially benefit from online retailing. Selling directly to the customer often gives a business the highest profit margins vs. brick and mortar distribution deals. Here are some of the major online retailing advantages and key benefits.

Lower business overhead and operating costs.

In comparison to getting a brick and mortar store started to retail, selling online is extremely cost-effective. Even with a marketing budget for the first 2 years, it is often still less than opening up a physical store. Online retailing is cost-effective, fast to launch, quick reach to the market, and the overhead and operating costs are minimal in comparison.

Greater sales reach and customer accessibility.

Retailing products online gives a business a much larger sales reach. At the same time customers have a greater experience and accessibility to products and services. E-commerce websites represent a brand 24/7, every day of the year, and worldwide. This would be hard to beat with a brick and mortar retail business.

Improved communications channels.

When retailing online, communication is often improved across multiple channels. Through email, chat, online forms, and the website brands quickly publish information streamlined. Online retailing allows brands to efficiently take orders, process shipments, payments, and communicate with suppliers, vendors, and potential customers.

Ability to integrate valuable reporting tools.

Online retailing allows for a complete integration of reporting tools such as Google Analytics, which provides statistics and critical metrics to retail successfully online. These tools make it very easy for business owners to gain valuable insights into their businesses.

To gain more insight into getting started with online retailing, entrepreneurs and businesses can obtain help through consulting services. A consultant can quickly shed light onto options and assist with tasks and processes. Consulting services enable companies to gain valuable insights prior to allocating money or making decisions.

Retailing online can be a lucrative business, when done right. Consultants can run all the right reports to gain the facts on demand, competition, and online opportunities for their clients. Clients get the facts prior to investing into retailing online. It is a more secure and safe method to get started with an online business and retailing online.

Traditional Retailing Stores

The commercial marketplace has evolved to the point where retail sales no longer have a monopoly on the consumer world. To elaborate, consumers once relied almost exclusively on retail outlets for their needed goods, but today you can purchase from online stores, auction sites, wholesale outlets, liquidation centers, and in some cases, you can even go straight to the manufacturer. If you sell any kind of merchandise, there are still advantages to using traditional retail outlets.

Customer Rapport

In a retail setting, customer rapport benefits both you as a buyer and a seller. Retail outlets allow customers to see what they are buying up close and, as opposed to online stores, they provide instant gratification, because the customer walks away with their purchases immediately. A friendly and helpful staff also helps to build customer loyalty, ensuring that customers return again and again. From a business standpoint, retail outlets allow you to reach a customer base that might be put off by the online marketplace.

Greater Inventory Options

When considering wholesale vs. retail, retail sales provides you with greater inventory options, because not all merchandise is available on the wholesale market. To provide a bit of perspective, wholesale goods come straight to the manufacturer to a wholesaler, usually mass produced at a low cost. The wholesaler may sell to a retailer or sell to the public directly. But because not all goods can be mass produced at a low cost, the wholesaler is limited in terms of inventory. By contrast, a retail business can produce goods for itself, purchase from wholesalers, or directly from manufacturers.

Greater Sales Potential

With a retail outlet, you can sell a variety of products and expose customers to items that they didn't even know they needed. For instance, a customer might enter the outlet looking for a pair of jeans, but then wind up purchasing jeans, three shirts, a belt and a tie. By consolidating a variety of merchandise in one central location, you dramatically increase your sales potential.

Less Drama

If deciding whether to sell in a retail outlet vs. online, consider that a retail outlet spares you from having to charge shipping costs and from having to deal with lost packages, tracking codes, customer addresses and complicated online sales databases. With a retail outlet, you can make each sale with greater confidence and fewer conflicts.

Benefits from Consumers

If you are a consumer and are considering reasons to shop at traditional retail outlets, as opposed to online, consider some of the same benefits. You can save on shipping costs, receive instant gratification, inspect your items carefully before making your purchase and not have to worry about packages getting lost in the mail. You also can have all of your questions answered immediately by helpful staff, rather than having to rely on email messages and phone calls.

Now I listed these two separately for a reason. You are now armed with knowledge to weigh in your own mind as to which route you want to go.

Regardless of my personal opinions about traditional retail stores, please don't allow that to sway your decision if that is the way you want to go.

There is one thing I will always remember that Alec Rodriguez said, "Entrepreneurs like minimum risk with maximum results." In other words, low risk, high reward.

References

Tanya Hall, August 2017. 5 Reasons You Should Start a Podcast
https://www.inc.com/tanya-hall/5-reasons-it-might-be-time-to-start-a-podcast.html

8 Benefits of using Youtube for Business. 2019.
https://wearegrow.com/8-massive-benefits-of-using-youtube-for-business/

Chris Cardell, 2019. 77 Ways to Get More Customers.
Benefits of Facebook for Business 2019.
https://www.business.qld.gov.au/running-business/marketing-sales/marketing-promotion/online-marketing/facebook/benefits

Benefits of Instagram Business, 2019.
https://business.instagram.com/getting-
started/?ref=sem_smb&utm_source=GOOGLE&utm_medium=fbsmbse
m&utm_campaign=G_S_Alpha_Instagram_Brand_US_EN_Acquisition_
General&kenid=0bfc92dc-7511-488c-9359-
1011b9098246&utm_content=benefits%20of%20instagram%20business
&product=NoDimensionAssigned&utm_keyword=benefits%20of%20inst
agram%20business&gclid=Cj0KCQjwu6fzBRC6ARIsAJUwa2QZHkJmlP
qPZo3R_Y5oLzMCr6nfu3oBy-_sBenVGa5lwSv_r6E-
Yc0NTgaAvlxEALw_wcB

Linkedin for Business, 2019. https://business.linkedin.com/marketing-
solutions/cx/17/06/advertise-on-linkedin?src=go-
pa&trk=sem_lms_gaw&veh=Google_Search_NAMER_USCA_Brand-
Head-
Terms_Beta_DR_AllLanguages_Restructure_378907683990__%2Blink
edin%20%2Bfor%20%2Bbusiness_c__kwd-
298952662303_6458957180&mcid=6612464045041733652&cname=G
oogle_Search_NAMER_USCA_Brand-Head-
Terms_Beta_DR_AllLanguages_Restructure&camid=6458957180&asid
=77594821136&targetid=kwd-
298952662303&crid=378907683990&placement=&dev=c&ends=1&gclid
=Cj0KCQjwu6fzBRC6ARIsAJUwa2TjKkLzeGmPbuPhZD6Vm5uzaB8Z_
ODj6NGLLofG8koqUkciTdCs56MaAjp8EALw_wcB&gclsrc=aw.ds

The Power of Twitter, 2019. https://business.twitter.com/

Naeem Dollie, Everything you need to know about Whatsapp Business,
April 2018. https://cleverclicksdigital.com/blog/everything-need-know-
whatsapp-business/

Valerie Peterson, 2019. What You Should Know About Being a
Published Author. https://www.thebalancecareers.com/being-a-
published-author-2799904

Jimit Bagadiya, 309 Social Media Statistics You Should Know for 2020,
2019. https://www.socialpilot.co/blog/social-media-statistics

Ginny Marvin, Amazon Is the Starting Point for 44% of Consumers,
2015. http://marketingland.com/amazon-is-the-starting-point-for-44-

percent-of-consumers-searching-for-products-is-search-losing-then-145647

Dorie Forbes, Stand Out, 2019. https://www.amazon.com/Dorie-Clark/e/B009FBO664/ref=sr_ntt_srch_lnk_1?qid=1469558803&sr=8-1?&tag=entrepreneurcom

Brian Halligan/Dharmesh Shah, Inbound Marketing, 2019 https://www.amazon.com/Inbound-Marketing-Revised-Updated-Customers-ebook/dp/B00MIT7ALS/ref=sr_1_1?s=books&ie=UTF8&qid=146954886 9&sr=1-1&keywords=inbound+marketing#navbar?&tag=entrepreneurcom

Josh Turner, Connect, June 2015. https://www.amazon.com/Connect-LinkedIn-Playbook-Relationships-Dramatically/dp/1619613271/ref=sr_1_1?ie=UTF8&qid=1468530774&sr=8-1&keywords=josh+turner+connect?&tag=entrepreneurcom

Jason Gaignard, Masterminds Dinners, 2019 https://www.amazon.com/Mastermind-Dinners-Relationships-Connecting-Influencers/dp/0692360026?&tag=entrepreneurcom

Mona Patel, Beyond Brainstorming, 2019. http://www.conversionconference.com/2016-agenda/reframework-workshop.htm

Edison Research, April 2018. https://www.slideshare.net/webby2001/the-podcast-consumer-2018

SoundCloud, 2019. https://soundcloud.com/

Internal Revenue Service, Deductions, 2019. http://www.irs.gov/Businesses/Small-Businesses-&-Self-Employed/Home-Office-Deduction

Hiring Your First Employee, 2019, https://us.accion.org/business-resources/articles-videos/hiring-your-first-employee

The Hartford, Setting Up an Office, 2020.
http://www.thehartford.com/business-playbook/setting-up-office

FedEx Business Grant Contest, 2020.
http://smallbusinessgrant.fedex.com/?cmp=AFC-1003834-2-4-SBGC

About the Author

Robert D Muhammad is a business owner and entrepreneur from Gadsden, Al.

He started Premier Leather Crafters in 1995, but only had mediocre success. It wasn't until 23 years later that he met his best friend , Kyle Hotaling, who led him to a meet and greet with Kevin Harrington, the original Shark, from Shark Tank, and the Inventor of

111

Infomercials. It was there that his entrepreneurial journey began. Over the past 6 years, under Kevin Harrington's mentorship, Robert has both flourished as a business owner/entrepreneur and a motivational speaker.

Through his unique style of inspirational and motivational speaking, he is one of the most requested speakers to new business owners and young entrepreneurs eager to hear his story.